AN ANTHOLOGY

AN ANTHOLOGY

Karachi
Oxford University Press
Oxford   New York   Delhi
1997

Oxford University Press, Walton Street, Oxford OX2 6DP

Oxford   New York
Athens   Auckland   Bangkok   Bombay
Calcutta   Cape Town   Dar es Salaam   Delhi
Florence   Hong Kong   Istanbul   Karachi
Kuala Lumpur   Madras   Madrid   Melbourne
Mexico City   Nairobi   Paris   Singapore
Taipei   Tokyo   Toronto
and associated companies in
Berlin   Ibadan

Oxford is a trade mark of Oxford University Press

© Oxford University Press, 1997

(copyright of individual poems remain with the poets)

ISBN   0 19 577814 6

Printed in Pakistan at
⟨E⟩ ELITE PUBLISHERS LIMITED
Published by
Ameena Saiyid, Oxford University Press
5-Bangalore Town, Sharae Faisal
P.O. Box 13033, Karachi-75350, Pakistan.

ACKNOWLEDGEMENTS

The publishers gratefully acknowledge the following publications for reproduction of poems in this book:

Shades of Silence, Sang-e-Meel Publications, Lahore, 1996.
Dowlite, Morning News, The Star, Leader, Mag, Holiday, Teenager, Woman's Own, Karachi.
World Poetry, India, 1983.
NE Europa, Luxembourg, 1987.
Teachers Forum, Karachi, 1996.
Portraits of Life, The National Library of Poetry, USA, 1996.
Poet, India, 1996.
Orbis, UK, 1991.
Verse, Scotland, 1992.
The Rialto, UK, 1992.
Iron, UK, 1992,
Cyphers, Ireland, 1995.
Poetic Page, USA, 1996, 1997.
Pax, USA, 1984.
The Sunflower Dream, USA, March 1997.
Firelight, USA, September 1997.
The Glow Within, USA, 1997.
Shade in Passing, Sang-e-Meel Publications, Lahore, 1991.
Escaping Twenty Shadows, Sang-e-Meel Publications, Lahore, 1995.
The Blue Wind: Poems in English from Pakistan, ed., Peter Dent, Interim Press, Devon, 1984.
Aspects: An Invitation to Free Thinking, Karachi, 1996.
Panchnad Industries Press, Lahore, 1995.

The contributing poets have confirmed that the copyright of their selection rests with them. Also they have provided the publisher with the names of the publications in which their work has appeared. While we have made every effort to ensure that this is correct, and to acknowledge all the journals in which the material has appeared previously, we apologize for unintentional discourtesy.

INTRODUCTION
Towards a Global English
Maya Jamil

New poetry in English written and published here is replacing the older poetry which was largely in the colonial tradition. In spite of the love-hate tie and new political and economic tensions, the writers are well aware of their heritage. Shahid Husain while editing *First Voices*[1] claimed that they had done justice to their heritage. Yet, at times, a sense of alienation can be felt, making this poetry different. This alienation, yet attachment, can be felt throughout however different the voices. Poets Ahmed Ali, Shahid Suhrawardy and G. Allana have been influenced by different languages, peoples and places. The Chinese influence is evident in Ahmed Ali and the French influence in Shahid Suhrawardy. These writers have come out of the 'Imperial Umbrella', creating a poetry of their own, handling the media with great mastery, yet not forming any distinct School.

Then, for a while, a dark period followed. People in Pakistan did not want to read poetry in English when they could read it in Urdu, Pushto or Punjabi. However, the poetic voice could not stiffled entirely. Poets continued to write, and a few such as Adrian Husain and Taufiq Rafat were published abroad, and won recognition, becoming guiding influences for the divergent streams that can be seen here.

Professor Manthrop in *Fifty Poems for Pakistan* says that poetry in English should be written by those whose first language it is, and who are rooted in that language. Taufiq Rafat states, however, that poetry should be written by

---

1. *First Voices*, Oxford University Press, Karachi, 1965.

those who are rooted in the earth on which it is written.

This earthiness, and the warmth and the vigour that it creates, can also be seen in the verve and zest of some of the contributing poets who have written with depth of passion and anger. On the other hand there are those who belong to a genteel tradition of the post-colonial period, believing in care, precision and exactness in every word.

This anthology consists of the work of poets, who have the right to 'be read and be published'. Busy in their respective professions, they are all actively contributing to the cause of poetry. The selection is varied and covers the work of some sixteen contributers. For some, this is the first time they are being published. Others are mature voices, having published individual volumes of work. Many of them have participated in poetry competitions both here and abroad and have won awards. Several have studied abroad and have been influenced by new poetry, proving that the world is becoming smaller, and that the move is towards a global English. Another new feature is the participation by poets of other languages—Sindhi, Pushto, Urdu, Punjabi—indicating that we have entered a different phase bringing to it a rich and varied heritage.

It is interesting and encouraging to see young poets making their presence felt. They are eager to exchange ideas. Some of the senior poets have come forward to listen to the new writers, hold discussions, and make suggestions. On the occasion of Pakistan's golden jubilee, Oxford University Press has recognized the need for a forum for both the senior and established poets, and also the young and lesser known writers. A beginning has been made for Pakistani poets writing in English.

CONTENTS

Shahryar Rashed

Sheryar Singha

Soofia Ishaque

Zeba Hasan Hafeez

KENT IN STOCKS

I, a modern Kent
with one foot in the stocks
feel terribly betrayed.

I do not recall betraying
my lord and king
or ever delaying the letters
from or to a sacred love
even for a moment.
I did not trip any
of Goneril's henchmen,
nor did I cross my path
with that witch, Regan.

I only recall night
on a black road
some grit in my mouth
and a pillar of flame
shooting from my kneecap
until the plunge in darkness.

If the wheel turned to this end
then I am happy with a foot in the stocks—
'sometime I shall sleep out:
the rest I'll whistle'.

LETTING IN

$\mathcal{I}$ am not often watching
from the window of your life
while passing by.
I am not always there
for one thing: only on
particular days when you display
your wet hairband or come
to wave a greeting or have
a brief chat do I see you.

It is up to you to open the window
a bit more—up to you to pass
or accept a plateful of hot food
through it.
It's upto you to show the dearly bought
finery of design and colour—
some colourful collage of the mind—
for my opinion; even
up to you to ask me to show
a corresponding vision with a smile…

But often I think
in a true neighbourly fashion:
how long will we keep this
contact level with the window-sill?
Won't you ever ask me to come up
at your life's doorstep—
and let me in?

CLASS CONSCIOUS

*W*ordcuffed in class
I sit in obedience
to the mute commander—
these dull pages who
have the power to

strike me dumb
snatch my words
even as they are uttered…
nothing I say is right
before the teacher
strikes at it with
an unbelievable violence—
as if my words are cotton fibre
let loose in the air
irritating the eyes and nose
or worse like the steady hum
of an insect near the ears
and then when I sit
word—and mind—cuffed
she blames my silence
as recalcitrant power.

I have yet to understand
your thralldom to this dull book:
what price in vitality
did you pay for it?
(Even if you did, why are you
asking us to pay it?)
What price was asked?
Or did you just assume
that without this discipline of

3

slavery to the book you will
not be counted among the free?
What costs in time did you
pay for this knowledge?
Do you know that it results
in a gagging of options...
each thing you say about
the words makes us see
the language less as joy
and more as a labyrinth
only the elect can manœuvre

But I will have some say
in the classroom crucible:
each thunderous put down
by you Teacher, I file away
and remember nothing escapes
    my assiduous attention:
These bare walls, these hard
benches, this unnecessary
poverty of mind and spirit
are all your sins for
which I will exact
an astonishing punishment:

I will stand up for
my rights with the
uprightness of innocence
and then my anger will flash
    like the Wrath of God.

ABBAS HUSAIN

POEM TO MY WIFE

$\mathcal{M}$y teacher said, 'Writing is a
provoked activity', and each letter
from you shows me this truth
with a distilled purity.
Perhaps distance is not enough
to provoke: perhaps my presence
was a short circuit which earthed
the surrounding electric world:
perhaps the shock waves beamed at you
make you too numb to write.

I say 'perhaps' my love because I
know this isn't so: my absence is
not that pain because I have yet
to let you in my sacred yard.
The stumps of my self-felled trees
of memories have their roots still deep...
so distance provokes this writing now
at a quaking moment of truth:

today, while changing clothes and
transferring my pocket contents,
I found that, among other trinkets,
I had your last letter—
(crumpled and folded and faded with touch)
and that it was with me always
like a talisman.

BHAKKAR TOWN

*W*hen mornings mean little, nights less
and days plod with sunny
regularity; when love or you press
one is tempted with sage-like brevity

to retreat where mountains leaf-fall
an inner wilderness.
There to sit cross-legged beyond recall
letting no water-time cliché profess

mutations but stay excesses.
In short, asceticize.
But being Bhakkar-bound, there are absences
for mountains, bushes for trees, compromise

and storms for cataracts, clouds. No
as far as all this goes
it's not conducive to uplifting. So
let alone the canal where buffaloes

splash with abandon; let alone this
bush which, summer dismissed
prompts an infinity's buried promise
following rain; let alone trees—jaundiced

to a pessimist—which dispense
yellow in dust-storms rough.
Only soft washes and settling silence
of the desert sunset are enough.

GURU

'*F*rom Punjab, through the Hind plains to Bengal
I have followed you, O *Nanak*, and seen
no man alive ever equal a small
quantum of your wisdom. Yet I have been

unable to decipher your words: when
one village drove us away, you blessed it
in your goodness. But the generous men
of the second village, you said, would split

and scatter. This has disturbed the heart, so and
clouded my mind.'
                          'Let it not burden you
O *Mardana* my minstrel, for when these

people disperse to distance, each will grow
as a seed and sprout to a tree and through
his goodness save hundreds from all disease.'

ELOHIM CREATING ADAM
after a painting by Blake

*H*old his head in your hands
and fill his features
with the emptiness of loneliness
and the will to disobey.

Now he lies outstretched
on the shores of an uncreated land,
mouth open, eyes sculpting
the unknown to what would be.

So let the sky darken Elohim
as on your muscled wings you sweep
across the clouds and the first sun.

There to unwind serpent darkness
for the reception of Adam.

SNAILS

South-East turns the compass of my thoughts
And I grope in a cracked niche.
Sometime in my morning, I had passed
That way. Now shadows lengthen, but
The smell of white sand beaches
The taste of pidgin English, and the
Song of the sarongs still lingers
On the receding waves of the sea.

I disliked snails then.
Behind each wavy motion
They left a liquid trail. Their antennae
Like two pins ready to prick themselves;
Their shells: mosque domes.
In my new found power
I had often crushed a few
And seen them wriggle to pulp.

Now, at this half erased touch, I recoil.
For under my comfortable skin
I see a snail.

TO A CHILD

Someone has jerked you out of sleep
Your one-sided unbroken peace with life.
And now, alarmed, not quite awake,
You think the world is on fire.
Fortunately that isn't the case.
Soon you will know and go back to bed
As sure of tomorrow as of yesterday.
But your dreams have given way to dragons
And fairies already are fairy tales.

TO A LADY
written on the tenth of Muharram

*T*oday you will let your hair down your back.
Today you will let your *chaadar* fall.
Today you will join the circle of women
Beating breasts, merging their pain
In the sufferings of those who
Chose to starve in the desert.
And give heads instead of hands, in hands
Demanding compromise.

You have often thought—whatever
There was to happen has happened.
'Birth—Copulation—Death'.
And what remains but to play back the video tape
Of time, and say at the end of
Each recaptured scene. 'It could have been so:
It should have been' and then.
'Anyway, it has and would have come to this'—

You have often wondered—
'What brought me to this Gibraltar.
And with what conviction did I
Burn all my boats?
In derision of what? And why am I here
All glittering to glorify my vanquisher?'

You have often longed to throw
An offered plate in a face.
And smear a smile:
To bite till disability
Fingers used to being gratified:
To vomit out each drop of

Milk, and wean a child—
As though you have tried and
Courage has compensated for such failures.
You have never cried.

Today you have found that ceremony of expression
Where grief is mistaken for pretence.
And pretence for grief.
You are safely stamped a hypocrite.
Today at the end of this mourning session
You will pray for a different kind of freedom.

PRAYER

I

Give me access to what I pursue
Not as soon as the first step is taken.
But after so much walking and knocking
That by the time I get there I forget my struggle
And consider it a miracle.

This constant condition of ability.
Giving, Making, Mastering, Self-Accordance, Shaping
                                                Life,
Might iconize my powers that are but wisps of Your
                                                Names.
So be Muhammad to my pride.
For I am when I suffer, and I'd rather be
Unidentifiable remains of an accident
Than a scarless sculpture piece.

Try me then,
Not as soon as this prayer is uttered.
But after some preparatory drills.
So that when it is time for the Great Test,
I stand at least a chance of success.

PRAYER

II

*F*or Thee do we worship and Thine aid we seek.
Grant us O Lord, in nights haunted with yellow-lion
dreams
After days wasted like their hooked marlins on seas,
The sword-surrounded sleep that takes its peace
In the thought of dying for the loved, the believed.

Grant us O Lord, in nights glow-wormed with Galahad
hopes,
After days Fausted with way-met temptations
The candle-quenching confidence that lets the loving
leave
Unembarrassed, unburdened, ungrudged.

For we yearn to be of those who shall neither fear nor
grieve.
And only Thee do we worship and Thine aid we seek.

MOHENJO-DARO, CITY OF THE DEAD

I

I wonder what this city was called before it died?
Before the Indus and the Himalayas were given names
When these bared streets, starved of people now,
Were flaring with the crested tumult of the living.

Uncovered by careful hands, brick by brick,
Where the mortar has turned to dust in between
Like the marrow in the anonymous bones.

Covered sewers, temples, baths, cloisters, courts,
Toycocks, figurines, gamesmen and sculpted busts,
Unearthed, catalogued, delivered of their aeonic rest
Each layer removed by the caress of brushes.

Metal ornaments, beads, sea-shells on rings,
Clay animals, stone weights, and red earthen pots,
Convoluted inscriptions and great-humped oxen
With ponderous heads and curving horns on seals.

II

There is a certainty in the citadels of power,
In the face of the priest-king, bearded, erect,
The true believer, scornful, sure as a rock.

The Earth Mother, comfortable and wide-hipped,
Disc-eyes staring, hypnotic and glacial,
Immune to the snares of reason or of doubt,
She would be eternally fecund, cornucopian.

15

The young dancing girl in bronze waiting,
One hand on her hip, the other arm covered
With metal bangles, jingling even at rest
And long black hair tied in a tight bun.

The pubescent body, stomach pouting a little,
Virgin, unused to loving, proud of being herself.
I saw her walking along her gypsy family cart
Of leather thong makers, legs smeared with mud.

III

In one grim room, skeletons lie criss-crossing
Arms and legs in tandem, as if caught in a game,
A stop-frame menagerie of sudden death.
It is difficult to believe in their humanity.

Fragments of ancient feeling recollected,
The necessary paraphernalia for the soul,
The patterns of joy, the geometry of love,
The bones of fear and dread, all sorted now.

Soon, shadows will spread like a flood
Of black waters across the sands
And the desert night will close
Its book on this once-city yet again.

IN SEARCH OF TRUTH AT THE GEOLOGICAL MUSEUM

*T*here's something of a place of worship
In a museum. The sapient ceilings reflect
The sombre sounds of reverence accrued.

Even the swirls of children scurrying in,
Ingest this and their scatter is muted.
Wonder tempers their ebullient pace.

Solemnly I stand before cages of glass
And learn that this febrile crust of earth
Is penny-stamp thin on a football globe.

The cake-layer crust is sliced, explained,
From ocean-brimming continental troughs,
Meeting the land's skinned desert hems,

Rising to the verdant renaissance of plains,
Gathering in upsurging snow-starched creases
In collateral quests, bristling with peaks,

Where the glaciers, grown monstrously,
Inch down, climbing one upon the other,
In laborious mating on haggard heights.

And the silver-sliver streams have trickled,
Three into two into one and disgorged,
Turbulent, thundering quick viciously,

Cutting their diamond-stylus courses,
Through grey mountainsides and
Through black rocks and ochre and red.

The frothing water has forged through them,
And saddened grudgingly into a river,
Meandering into loops, wide and silted.

I stride to the Earthquake Machine.
The calm of endless charts and diagrams
Belies the simmering chaos that churns beneath.

PHOTOGRAPHY

*C*hildren playing with knotted movements
Of brittle limbs like bare branches
After a drought, coated in flour dust,
Their bellies distended, being maimed
Irrevocably in the clean country air.

I try varying angles and distances,
Looking for the right expressions of pain
In their faces, in their expectant eyes.

They smile at me and are shy, unsure
About a camera and what it can do,
With the glass eye in its fat nose.

It is not like a gun, they know,
It makes no sound and does not kill.

For a moment they stand almost still,
Hiding behind each other, laughing.

Why are they always covered with flies?
There is no food in them. I compile
The scant traces of their flickering lives,
Knowing they are, and will remain,
Themselves food for predators of all kinds.

GHULAM FARIDUDDIN RIAZ

LEAF FALLING

*T*hree floors down the naked cars
Bank the neon street in queues.

The night owl autumn trees
Filled with purple sky, and I,
Echo the gaunt twists
Of our several losses,
In the stark spaces
Between high brick walls.

A small leaf drifts
Down through the air,
Entirely golden, completed,
Ready for other uses now.

There is not the slightest
Whisper of a breeze, or
Any other complaint. It falls,
Falls and is lost among others
On the grass, aflame
With red orange hues.

There was no mystery
Encapsulated in the fall
Of that frail descending form,
All that passed was time
From branch to earth to eye.

I resolved, yet again, to learn,
To live, on the brink of stillness
Within the private spectrum of
Unimportant happenings, convincingly.

20

THE SILENCE

*T*here were mountains in my past,
Where seasons met
In the layered cinema of leaves,
Where the swelling wetness
Of the boulders and tree trunks
Gave shelter to our covenants.

Perilous crags escape the earth
Where once our footprints
Left pockets in the grass,
And the hawk clatters downhill
Along the contours of denuded hills.

The silence fluctuates grimly,
And questions turn darkly around
To ask who took what from whom
And who dwindles at the core,
Blinded by a collapsing sky.

CHIMERA

*B*equeathing the shimmering earth,
With a multiplicity of shapes,
Time has transversed me,
Like the smithereened light
Of an angry sun, pouring
On the brows, in the hollows
Of a furling, brewing stream.

Infused with a current,
Stirring the quaking air,
I know I am someone, briefly.

And in the lot of my soul,
Silken in eyeballs,
Lives the harlequin,
Mime for all seasons,
Chimera electric—
Always transforming me,
Yet always me.

Look within me,
Where sadness is my dawn,
I change, I am the same.

ALEXANDER COMES OF AGE

*H*e had not winced when the Sphinx made no reply,
The pangs of immortality were so acute, so manifest.
Fulfilling his destiny he strode across the earth,
And then as proof positive the late great Darius lay,
Finery in tatters, plumes awry, jewels snatched away,
Smothered in blood and sand, conclusively betrayed.

He relished the feast of Empire, single-mindedly,
As hosts of lesser Kings, Princes, Lords and Khans,
With impeccable traits of wealth and valour
Were brought to heel. Surely he had surpassed Achilles?

It was on Jhelum's banks the magic began to shred.
First, Bucephalus, died. The horse-god with harness
And horns of gold, who was to gallop to eternity
On the evergreen flower-laden flanks of Olympus,
Ended inconstantly in the dust like any other horse.

Battered by wars, the Companions rebelled at the Beas,
Denying him the glory of standing on the edge of Earth.
In Multan an arrow struck deep into his chest, irrev-
                                        erently.
Piercing his lung, it gave him his first shudder of death.
The capricious sun to which he had so often sacrificed
Devoured his armies in the desert furnaces of Makran.

In Hamdan, a passing fever killed his love, Hephasthion,
And not since he had killed Clietus in a drunken fit
Had he known such anguish. He wept inconsolably for
                                        weeks,
Adrift from life, away from Roxane, from touch.
Each day the wound worsened, festering in his mind.

23

After that he seldom felt like a god or even lion-like
And in intense moments of regenerate invincibility,
When he saw conquests ripened everywhere,
He would consider plucking Arabia, Africa or Italy,
But fell back to wearing Babylon like a stolen mantle
And drank himself, feast after feast, to oblivion.

He would not, could not remember how many corpses
Of nobles, captains, friends, devotees lay strewn
On random plains, in deserts, in forests and gorges,
In alleys and on the blood stained walls of citadels,
Or drifted in steaming rivers, bloated, to the sea.

THE WITCH OF POVERTY

*G*irl, webbed with poverty, dried inside
Like a wrinkled date, ancient
As a rock-riven mountainside,
Benumbed, ravelled, cleft and cloven.

Where do I begin to unravel you?
Knotted, weft and warp so fine,
Closed to common feeling.
Cleft like a stick
With no paleness or blueness
Of sky or waters in between the lines
Of your mind. Cloven like a hoof.

The hunger that has stained the underside
Of your being makes you untouchable.
I pray that your emptiness be stirred
And you cry out loud with feeling.

There are no answers, only the possibility of loving,
Which softens hides as tough as rocks and dissolves
The thorns of fear strewn by the witch of poverty.

FULL MOON IN A MUD-WALLED COURTYARD

*I*t is your hand that has linked
Lost lyric ends to the sharp scent
Of fresh beginnings.
A memory of soft voices
Under the high branches of a *neem* tree,
A sun-dappled face upturned,
Which resurfaced like a sudden breeze
From the hinterland of past images
To recreate the rites of pain.

Who asked for certainty? I did.
You are far more courageous
Than me. You despise certainty,
You believe only in this day's sun.
I am a collector of wooden moments,
I need too many walls to cover
With the images of all my yesterdays.

And yet who is to know that you are not
A collector of yesterdays as well?
May be at heart you are like everyone else.
Just as capable of love, of needing love,
That in your innermost being you too
Are looking for permanence, the hearth,
For a full moon in a mud-walled courtyard,
To hoard the bright night between walls,
Awaiting a tomorrow that will linger forever.

PRISONERS OF MEMORIES

*W*eep for all the women raped during war and peace
By soldiers, priests, paupers and princes alike
Who felt no shame crushing innocents, inflicting pain

Monsters forget their mother's encircling arms
The flow of paradisical milk, its life loving taste
Their sins of strength dishonour fathers, tribe and race

The beasts of Nature nurture, sustain and honour their
own
Conscience—blind humans torment their own, devils
weep
Even beasts are shocked witnessing Man's disgrace

Prisoners of piercing memories, cannot kill memory
Only death demolishes their innermost secret agony
Girls, women never raped, be glad you escaped

Presidents, premiers, parliaments of the earth
Women raped challenge your powers to eliminate
Monsters who rape the peace, the progress of the land.

THE TWENTY-FIRST CENTURY: OPTIONS

Weapons Desires

The weapon barons think of chemical confusion
The biology engineers plan genetic grandeur
The nuclear neurotics calculate the first strike

The computers are in distress
The questions are hopeless
The answers they suppress

The chorus of cockroaches sings
The pesticides are obsolete
The earth is our domain we remain

Earth Dreams

The butterflies celebrate the rainbows
The humans damned their weapons
The earth people sleep and wake without fear

The flowering trees scatter their fragrance
The arts and sciences bestow on LIFE abundance
The frontiers of knowledge expand minds ascendant

The oceans and skies boomerang with peace
The rose reveals its innermost secrets
The weapons are DEAD devoured by PEACE

THE RAPE OF MACHARANWALI[1]
dedicated to women who are victims of crime

Death Cry:
Land of my fathers and their mothers
Clothed with proud Begs and silk scented Begums
Broadcasting grand Commissions, Forums, Ministries
We are the daughters of a naked land
Bring us the ashes of our garments from Macharanwali

Consolation:
Sisters of my naked land
The Indus weeps dry for Macharanwali

Second Cry:
Mothers of my naked land
Be wombless for Macharanwali

Question:
Women of my cotton rich land
Who are you of Macharanwali

Answer:
We are dead and living in you, you and you
We are all the names—Nawaban, Sardaran, Faqiran
And all the names of daughters, sisters, mothers
Ask of your sons, brothers, fathers
Can they not wipe out Macharanwali

Question:
Where is *Chaddar* and *Char Devari* [2]
Homeless in Macharanwali

---

1. Representative of all places where crimes of rape have been committed.
2. Veil and home.

Have the cotton mills collapsed
On naked Macharanwali

Answer:
Favour us in the naked land
Bury us tenderly in Macharanwali
They speak of *Adalat* and *Insaaf*[3]
We beg only for *Kaffan*[4] Macharanwali

Question:
Why talk of dying Macharanwali
Hear the shamed voices of men and women wailing
For your pain, impossible to revenge Macharanwali

Answer:
No, we of the naked land hear not
The lamentations, proclamations of our Rights
From the Halls of many splendoured Conferences
High Ministers soft Secretaries, loud leaders of the Land
Your feet and eyes touched not Macharanwali
And tall shadow Ministers, your shadows
Fell not to soothe the disfigured of the naked land

We are the forsaken of Macharanwali
No this is now raised to *Bichuanwali*[5]
To be next elevated to *Sappanwali*[6]
Leave us alone in the naked land

---

3. Courts and justice.
4. Shroud
5. Land of scorpions.
6. Land of snakes.

Passive Confession:
We hear your silent screams Macharanwali
YOU protect us in the naked land
Release us from our promises, oaths, words of honour
Forgive us our actionless cowardice, words of courage
Of Yesterday, Today and Tomorrow
Find your own salvation, Oh Macharanwali

Third Cry:
Yes fly away untouched by our dying flames

Active Response:
We salute your pain martyrs of Macharanwali
Your voice and words strengthen committed hands
Brave men and women continue to struggle for just
                                                change

Down centuries through corridors in bleeding chains
You have survived Macharanwali kept alive the race
Monuments of your sacrifice will not be erased
Accept Macharanwali our individual collective shame

We have no gifts Today, Tomorrow may reverse
Your fate our fate with determined hands and hearts,
United to defeat the enemies of Humanity
Hope lives to witness your rebirth Macharanwali

STILL LIFE

*C*eramic sky
chipped with branches
and a few still birds,
carefully patterned.

You rearrange
thought after thought
in the blue vastness
that will not go away.

MANSOOR Y. SHEIKH

PEARL

*W*hat mad colours of pain
what stale ecstasies
of rhythm
does the sea endure in us

it is almost winter again
and the lights of grey ships
spill and unspill
in the water

to be alone at this hour
to stagger alongside
moondappled waves
and then stop

and find in the night
a niche for respite

SHALIMAR

*W*hat abandon
filling these pools of stone
where jewelled fingers
once caressed their own reflections:

moon-bathed pavements
where you can still
sense a footfall
or an occasional *sitar* crescendo

from the bedchamber.
Yet they do no take you
through the inflexions of time
to where the music swells and nights falter.

WORDS STOOD IN SLAVERY

*Y*ou came like the sudden shower of rain
To an arid land on a summer afternoon
Bringing a whiff of spring, a lease of life
For the sun-singed leaves—
The desert bloomed with a thousand lotuses

All faces dissolved into one
All voices lost in whispers.
Your passion-starved lips blazed
Into a thousand tongues of fire
And eyes radiated with the unspoken, the unspeakable
To which a million words stood in slavery.

A FORTRESS FOR THE SPIDER QUEEN

*N*ot long after you slighted the gift I gave you,
I cursed you with the fury of ancient gods
Not fully realizing how the wrath of my words
Could denude you and erode the beauty of your face
How the rose and the fire that bloomed and blazed
Would turn to singed petals and trifle ashes;
My tears of regrets cannot restore your beauty
Nor recall your lost, triumphant youth;
No Lucretia Borgia, how could you afford
To disregard with arrogance the tribute of a poet,
A toiler of words, a creator of world beyond world?
Nemesis, the lame goddess, has limped her way to you
And holds you prisoner in the purgatory for the damned
You have your wages now, your remorse cannot undo
The havoc you wrought upon the poet's world;
As each grain of sand runs in the hour-glass,
Your hell begins anew—each particle of sand
Brings a fresh spasm of agonies,
You re-live your sins as you re-run through
The phases of your life from the beginning to the end
Where lies your triumph now, where flows the venom of
                                                    pride?

You rule now the empire of sack and ashes—
Your palace, a ramshackle of crumbling bricks.
No prince or poet with baited breath will kneel
To have a fleeting glimpse of what once was your face
No man will bear to have you by his side
But you can still turn for rescue and retreat
To the poet's fort that once you chose to spurn.

CHRYSANTHEMUM BLOSSOMS

*T*he desert spreads
Not even a cactus grows
Only the memory of your face survives
You are chrysanthemum and lily and rose
The rest are grains of sand
Where life cannot even struggle
To maintain so much as a tenuous existence.

Your eyes persuade me
And your voice haunts my ears
In waking and in sleep
I lift my hands to offer a feeble prayer
To protect the beauty of the lily
The odour of chrysanthemums
The sanctity of the rose
What can a poet do but attempt
To build a sanctuary of word
Where the beauty of your face
Remains unravaged by the havoc
Of hungry eyes that rivet on you
Within the ramparts of my words
Your sweetness and your youth
Shall remain unassailed, unwrecked
You exist in me like the fragrance of spring
Like bloodstream in the veins
Life has never been easy without you
The emptiness, the void corrodes me
I have struggled to sustain these desert years
The cactus years—the hopelessness, the lost efforts.

Your face survives the ravages of autumn
Be with me when the wind blows wild

And shatters my being and unsettles my repose
Your occasional smile resurrects my buried youth
Redeem these moments of ennui and grief
Let the lotus bloom and flowers blaze forth their tongues
of fire

How shall I rebuild my gossamer empire
To retrieve the beauty of the lost moments
The chrysanthemum garden of your wild embrace?
Or shall I sing a litany of autumnal sorrow
At the gathering storm that seeks my extinction?

A PRAYER FOR THE DISILLUSIONED

*S*o, finally the master-mason has abandoned
The city you thought he had built for you.
I could read thousand schemes written on his face:

The discreet silence, the misleading smile—
But I chose not to speak then;
Time has unrolled the hidden scroll.
It hurts me to see your gradual destruction
Like the dream-house falling brick by brick—

The master-builder has chosen to construct
Another city, for his world is elsewhere.
Do not therefore despair or turn sour
To the world at large. It isn't the end
Of the world yet. You must now travel
From the city of memory and desires
To another city where love abounds
Where peace descends in dew drops.
It pains me to see you stand in the labyrinth
Of the ruined walls and roofless complexes—
A living testimony of the ruthless architect.
I had foreseen the death of the city
But such passion you nourished
For that dream-city that I dared not
Foretell its doom before you.
I lift my hands in prayers to the Lord of the Universe
To demolish all illusory cities
And rebuild on its ruins a paradise for you.

YOUR BEAUTY NEEDS NO TRIBUTE

*A*s you sat before me
I was struck by the beauty of your face
Your hair dark, dishevelled
And the stars of your eyes—
You took my breath away
I thought I should craft words
Of prophyry and pearls to capture your beauty
Words elude me, they slip, they crack
For your beauty is beyond words—
Past the sculptor's skill

Perhaps your beauty remained
Unrevealed to the world's eyes
For you had no Homer or a Yeats to sing your praise
But is the fleur-de-lis the less beautiful for blooming
unknown?
How can I frame your face in a rhapsody of phrase
I therefore offer these frail words at your feet
For the gods themselves have given their verdict
On the divinity that is you.

LOST VOICES

Summer's dying:
the first breath of winter,
like a stubborn song,
brings back your truth.

An ancient wind seeps through pores
rescuing images of beings
conjoined from seasons past.

The city has streets we drew with our feet,
outlines of meanderings into another life.
That same smell, the smoke of our rickshaw,
its staccato sounds shattering
trysts of silence with memory.

The old house has windows
which exhale lost voices.
Vestibules reverberate
with sounds from the ante-room,

Where you once lay,
feeling winter with your skin.

GRAVES

Names speak from marble slabs
recalling hands that spoke
and mouths that kissed and maimed.

The keeper sprinkles rose water
on the sleeping.
There are ants scurrying inside little holes
in bones, black lives feeding
on vapours of memory.
Tombs of earth speak of regeneration.

The keeper takes ten rupees to recite
the praise of the Lord,
the prayer for refuge from sin.

Mourners toss fistfuls of dust
on the sealed vault. They cleanse their faces
with the earth and smell the coming
season of rains and laughter.

LIST OF DAMAGED AND DESTROYED MONUMENTS

Near the gaunt, unshaven faces
under the dome of falling shells
they lie scattered,
bricks perspiring centuries
on backs of masons wailing
in blackened vaults:

the mosque in the village Drinsko near Vishegrad,
the Church of St Pelar and Pavao,
the Kozluca Mosque in Zvornik,
and the Madrese of Mehmed Pasa Kukavica in Foca; ‹

and the roll call marches on
of echoes in halls silently falling
beside the once-living
with all the alien pleasure of names tortured
off the tongue;

names for stones and foreign souls
now going,
now gone.

LIFE OF THE IMAGINATION

So much is left to the imagination,
Dreams and their coming true,
The love once sought acquired,
Places visited that really do not exist.

It is tiring and full of ennui
for the body to feel no pain.
Only the mind reacts, argues,
Laughs and loves. The body merely

Draws the map of the intellect's
Fancy wanderings. The latitude and
Longitude of an event on the
Horizon of possibility. Cry,

The tears are scratch marks;
Laugh, the sound is echo to a profile,
Seen like some mist solidified into
A talking person. Only when love

Intervenes, much as the inevitable
Wall of all lives, do the bounds appear.
The circular logic of fancy reveals
The inner limit of body and soul.

PARTITION

*I*n that year
they left the old house
taking the odour of clothes
and souls.

We replaced the trees and crows,
and planted fresh birth sounds
and sleep sounds.
We changed nameplates.
We changed the street.

Even now when the pot boils
on the old stove
making tinny sounds,
it is the noise of the morning women
restless, and the men
demanding bread.

There is cement on sandstone,
concrete on the ground
where the sleeping desert
once swam.

But from the cracks in walls
the house speaks.
There is breath
coming from the black loam
around the rose bush.

The ants speak
The wind that slaps the west wall
speaks.

I can smell the master's dream
in his old white vessel
soiled and tattered,
holding the bricks of the wall.

Shadows of bones walk
in the night.
The house bares its soul
with each monsoon drop
on the window-sill.

THE CROWS

*I*n the mango tree in the backyard
she planted when she was just married,
there are crows cawing, crying for blood,
calling, calling.

Mother never cried,
though her tears were moist foliage.
The crows were never hungry;
she fed them meat and bread from our mouths
as sacrifice.

In the heavens there was a blue temple
she called to. The temple spoke;
there were comforting voices for her.

I thought I saw ice on her lips
when they showed her death face.
The crows flew overhead in droves.
They cried for her;
they paid homage.

The day she went we buried the world
and inscribed the dead sun on her gravestone.

THE RETURN

*A*fter washing Paddington loos
and scrubbing Hampstead streets
I returned to my piece of the Punjab
bought the twenty-six acres they took
from my father,
dry, hot land
that stopped giving birth to dreams the day
he died in a London hospital, his *lungi*
covering his bony face till eternity

Now the land is giving birth again
it cries every season
with new voices, and the stars
rain down white light again
   but the men still come
   looking for *kafirs,*
   unbelievers
Two days ago another died
they called *kafir*
(My old man said to me:
'I can see, but I am willing to be blind')

On nights when the air is choking with dust
and heat
I close my eyes and place
my hand on the soft, pregnant
belly next to me
and I remember the green hills
of *Inglistan*
   and the boot steps that
   one dark night followed me

in a drunk and sour London alley
calling
kafir! kafir!
(And my old man said to me:
'I can see, but I am willing to be blind')

CHACHI

*C*hachi, the aunt,
was no longer playing dead.
She went dreaming
She was writing another poem,
Her hands creaky and stiff.

Her face—a dark, dried fruit,
A black raisin enveloped in white
When they opened it the last time to show the bereaved
Who are witness to her passing—
was not hers.

Her notebook had eyes.
It flapped in the soft breeze of the veranda,
On the chair where she sat,
with her thick lenses tapping on its cover.
That is the aunt:
Behind the black 1952 frames
That framed her raisin face like a hyper-realistic painting,
and the writing in the book,
the blue-black blanket of ants,
alive and moving.

LOOKING BACK FROM THE COLD

*W*e stuffed our mouths full of
William the Conqueror and hot cross buns,
scenes of a little English village
a dream as real as the sun.

Timothy, the boy from the book,
who went exploring on the heath and caught the gang
was an ordinary boy I thought I'd like to know
if only I knew where England was.

(Mrs Shaikh, the cynical Englishwoman married to
                                        Pakistan
correcting, 'Plummer, not plumBer, you stupid boy!')

When I came home from school I taught Jamil,
the cook's son, how to sing doe-a-deer
and we both laughed at his singing,
insensitive to times not spent together,

drifting apart, he into sand and earth,
and I into the dung of imagination,
with Lord Nelson vanquishing the Spanish.

Father looked from his sterile corner,
lost in a bygone world
of *ghazals* and dancing girls,
lost in Lucknow which he lost to us.

Our universe now is square, neat,
electronically filtered,
uncluttered by an old man squatting in dirt for his toilet,
or a woman raising a fistful of food to her mouth.

We took the short cut to decency,
crossing the mind's barrier to another world.

On moist days the face sometimes feels
odd to be here, in unwelcome cold;
the cold makes the past ring:
a forgotten sun, a bearded man praying,
the girl on the porch waving...

All dead now,
buried under a metalled distance.

MONA HASSAN

FOOTLOOSE

There I've thrown all care to the winds
  And I've let myself go once again!
They come and ask me what I do;
What strange cult do I pursue
  And I tell them I have found myself again.
Waves are thrashing in my ears and
  All my heartstrings are thundering again!
All my twines and aches are through
I would like to tell them too
  Though I defy them, I've learnt to live again!

A VOID

Why not give each other space?
I do not need you so much—
Sometimes sleeping pills would do
To blunt the pain;
Sometimes newspapers, books and others people's lives
Are quite enough
To keep me in good spirits;
Propriety and other such menaces
Keep me away;
And then there are your natural vices,
Your unfathomably cruel devices;
There are reasons enough
For women of my sort;
I can think; I can rationalize;
I can be quite self possessed…
For hours at a time.

MY FOSTER GOD

*M*y man you are an infant
Fresh from your mother's womb
What do you know what a woman is?
Go on Ulysses fight your battles
Upon the fields of Troy
Make your presence felt
You will return a victor, no doubt
Glory will be yours
And an ego big enough
To embalm, your Penelope

We are a poor people, my love,
And when you come home
I can offer you no meat
No fresh butter, no sweets
Fit for a victor's feast
There is only this yeasted bread
Which I have saved
Even from my own children
To give to you
And only this tattered cloth
And only this hardened floor
To sleep on
And these resounding walls
Where I sweat and dust
And bear you child after child

There are no doors
Which open the world to me
Only the one from which
You make your exits
No sound reaches here

Except the cries of my children
And the falsetto of your steps approaching
In this bleak room where
I gasp for air
Would you deny me air, my foster god?
Then be it so; for in this room
Life is condensed
Throbbing, kicking and screaming
With my children...

PRINCE SALIM'S REGRET

*G*ardens, songs and marble courts are nothing.
A rose does not smell,
As once it did, of love;
I take to pleasure
To keep away the hurt
And yearn in secret for a wink of sleep.

When will sleep come? Since you have gone away
These nights have grown long;
I walk in guilt as if
They cling to me still,
Your jasmine and roses;
All my manhood is buried in some wall.

Cowardice? Ambition? What does it matter now?
What will reasons bring?
What good will prayers do?
Only memories console
And memories sting,
The cleansing acid of memories.

Go away. Do not haunt me this way.
Who knows what love is?
What is that we call sin?
I loved a dancing-girl...
And we sinned. That's it.
Praises to the court of Akbar the King!

DEATH BEFORE LIFE

A tiny ray of hope
Tiptoed in
Hoping no one would spy him.
But keener ears
Heard the footsteps
And made off with him.
I watched it all
With despair in my heart
And I remained
As ever.
Empty–handed.

POEM

I

*D*ark days
and darker nights
were one
till
you came
making the darkness
a forgotten memory
for I now live in light.

But darkness didn't forget me
stealthily   ;
one day he walked in
and sweet-talked you
into going with him.

Turning a deaf ear to my pleadings
you walked out of my life
and I was alone once again.

But darkness—
moved by I know not what
sent you back to me
and I once again live in light.

POEM

II

*S*urrounded by invisible walls
afraid
a loving touch
would
in a moment
destroy walls so carefully built
leaving you open to the cold
unfeeling fingers of the world
you
shut everyone out
even
your own self.
yet
for a moment—
a few heartbeats?
all eternity?
you found in yourself the courage
to reach out
and with a simple gesture
open yourself
and let love flow.

POEM

III

Sleep-heavy eyelids
dipped
half-moon shadows darkened the cheeks
and you slept.

CHASMS OF FEAR

*I*n melting darkness
of dying light, slow—and grey
despair in desolation
with no promise of peace.
Souls staked high in a
whirling fire of effacement;
determined by their own secret pathos.
Recollections on a face ravaged yet vibrant,
'I hold my sorrow rather well', she said,
this woman from Kashmir, Bosnia or Chechnya
with a simple, yet, sacred independence.
What survives, grieves: weaves after thoughts,
Only one feat is possible—not to have run away
from the dark adits of the soul
an arête between chasms of fear.
Life is measured by the living—
by the moon-rages of the burning heart,
by the burning and turning of
the trembling heart...
by assault on a wave of light
through wounds made
on the horizon's edge
in the chill of night
lit in a haze of stars.
When the body burns away its dross
when the soft-skin film of silence
shatters to flailing-flames
striving for liberation!
Never to remain at the cross-roads
but to take a path—beyond ourselves.

...IN PATHS OF PAIN

*D*o we know, what we know?
of shades of silence,
in paths of pain—the
searing sadness in the far reaches of the soul.
Do we know?
of those who have been to the edge of
emptiness. Where the mind retreats
to calloused crypts in cruel baptisms of fire!
Days, slow in an endless wilt
the night will not caress,
nor caulk the pain of
valediction!
Sorrows accrete,
tenderness erodes in
eyes lucent with grief.
The endless recall of
severance,
fossilled on the mind of
time.
Do we not build on memories of love? from passages of
childhood, across aeons of
time, revisit the doorless
barriers of light!
Can we not hear
the keening of mangled-hearts?
Sorrows liming the mind
in still illusion.
   The quest is endless,
time, we looked unto
others souls—effete, febrile
purged of the self...
the grey abyss, spawns

the primal beginnings
to the lone descent.
   From shades of solitude
let us build the
silent shrine of love.

THE RECALL

*I*f you came this way,
this way of the transitory blossom
in a spring-time of promise
blanched into a summer fading,
with soul-steeped love.
If you arrive at all
with stricken heart
you will find the end
that you seek, has changed
its meaning; the purpose altered.

For you walked too long
alone, in the waning dusk
forgotten, half-recalled
too strange for misunderstanding
and I stood
shelterless alone
in the shaded haunts
of recall, grieving
while my heart
ran circles
searching for you.

HOMING

*T*his land of my birth
This land, whose intensities
prime my blood;
this sanctuary, half-forgotten
where time began for me.
The roots go deep,
in the sun-warm'd
wind-blown earth
hands crusted its richness
on cheeks; built mud-cak'd huts
of dreams,
on burnt rose leaves; soft-blown
jasmine scented, the air
I breathed,
wove, unwove, memory—webs
ineluctably twined in fading dusks
amidst a prickling of stars.
The world then was horizontal
lustrous green, trailing
dew-lanes on flower leaves
falling motes filtered, sieved…
fireflies on moon lit palings:
foliage essences of earth exhalings,
here nothing was scanted.
But ecstasies are brief: visions fade
of ineffable sweetness
a moments rime, on the
cross-winds of time.
Slowly yet,
slowly the dusk grew
shadows festered
The musk rose, consuming…

at this intersection of timelessness.
To you, I return
ever and always
you are to me
a homing—an expanding of love
beyond wantingness
beyond liberation.

FRACTALS OF THE MIND

In the furtive conspiracy of
dawn, a silence replete
and awesome; when pale
intrusions of hope dissolve
and certitude destroys the mind,
a voice cries out in agony,
and dies unattended,
guilty on suspicion.
In antinomies
of thought and deed
of violated visions; and truths immured
we traffic in mockery, the soul
waylaid by moil of ages.
We talk; we take but not
communicate and blaspheme unheard
in a life alliterative
with mediocrity.
Visit the inscape; the fractals
of the mind—a manageable
chaos
of musings, dreams and
strangeness
illumined, crossed, re-crossed
by errant lights
countering the negative gravity
of sorrow spaces.
Soul sediments settle
a crimson flower grows
in scarlet flickers of
tissued flame…
life burns a flamier-flame
what lies deeper than despair

than despair itself?
In slow deepening darkness
a tree branched in cries
of silence; stronger than thunder
stares at the skyline
in indifference.

KASHMIR

*I*n silence began
a striving—slow metamorphosis
of hidden realities, sifting, separating.
To re-dream, re-emerge
amidst heat-bursts,
in dusk-peppered evenings
plucking strange dirges of
anguish; resonating, cleaving the air,
flaming proclamations of the suffering heart.
The endless permutations of
love to be incarnated
in Kashmir—flame-blossoms
in bloodstain'd streets
and desecrated shrines,
strange assonance of fear
the silence of petrified years
yielding to the muted
misted calls of birth.
One must unlearn; how to die,
quell the dissonant, inconsolable
wail, glooming away to an
attenuated end. To survive
the moon-rages of the
circling spirit, caught
between eternities
of race, of soul.
Touched by mellowed
whispers of the sun,
a green chaos,
a miracle of boughs,
children wild-eyed, wonder-bound
do they even know

what it is all about?
Tread warily with pilgrim-feet
in wooded vales and
shadows deep,
with home, half-forgotten
in alien lands.
In the susurrant whiteness
of dawn,
in the whatness of the hour
not to grieve; rather hoard
the strength of the
unchanging heart.

BEYOND THE VEIL

𝒩ever to him come
never hear the cries of those
creatures of light; who paint
arabesques of faith hope tenderness,
yet, sequacious follow
the mindless tyranny
of insensate beings—
which is a death
beyond the veil.
A lone face, calm in her grace
she sat,
while skeined transparencies
of thought traced
fire-patterns in her being.
A legacy of humilations!
sully her soul,
rived flesh, bared to the indignities
of human callousness.
Let us talk of bondage to
enlightened man.
Let us talk of slave trade,
of inequality—of being cast aside
in the emptiness
of the night.
Let us talk of the
despair in her eyes!
The hand that lit the lamp
rough with labour
her calloused soul.
What of the hope
in those henna'd palms
raised in prayer—

to die, yet many deaths
await the desecration
of the innermost sanctuaries
of her mind.

BACK TO THE CAVES...?

*T*he Margallas silent
swathed in heat-light
a green haze, emerald leaves
ablaze. Breathlessly,
the sky cruel, clean as slate.
Memory-less.
A névé of emotions
involute, curling, curling
to dark ebony essences
in primeval silence.
On polished stone
lizards slither; a ledge
or an edge; to cower
under or go over?
heat-murmurs in the noon-day sun
what must come: must come.
What matters most, mostly matters
not. It is a choice.
Between the caring and
uncaring; the human
and humane; lies a thought.
What are those words?—
inequality, deprivation, hunger—
human sores healed by
forgetfulness. Amnesia
is a blessing. They say.
What of despair? Face-glows
vague as fog-mists…
moon-rushes on the Jhelum.
Will the nightingale sing itself hoarse?
I wonder—the negligence and
poverty, is it in our stars?

Can we deny the singing in our bones?
Shards of shattered earth—
the crust rich with promise,
this handful of devotion, to efface
oneself, be empty, utterly empty
in a blaze of peace!
Shall we say enough is enough
turn loose,
our sorrows.
Shall we go then,
back to the caves?
Or sit here endlessly
chasing shadows; gathering
dusk in the troubled shade.

SARAJEVO

Shards of sunlight
shredded on grave-heads
wantonly, lit with
grief.
Motes of light shimmer
and spill on dank leaves;
serrated shadows
dark and light
move in empathy
with souls transfigured in sorrow.
Will their dreams
ever blur the intransigence of fate?
What strange evocations
bring us sadness born of Truth.
These closures of the mind,
cannot comprehend
the glow-worms of pain,
mute gestations of love,
buried hilt-deep
in the flesh,
mutating, evolving, faceless and silent.
Beleaguered city!
We mourn thy living.
Mists hung heavy on hearts
that do not care anymore…
Ravages of hate, or is it the futility of time?
Encapsuled, weaving terrible webs of
knowledge.
Will we ever hear the silent wail?

UNION

Soft skin enmeshed in mine,
How fine a net we wove together
Amid the sea,
Through endless time,
Upon the beach, beside the brine
The waters wash ashore.
Like trees entwined
Against the breeze,
The foam that rises from the sea,
The sun that melts in earth at dusk,
You are the corn and I the husk.

A DIALOGUE ACROSS GENERATIONS

I see you now as you were when
The sun cast gold on your brown bent
Head. Dipping your soft white hands in
Dyes of deep, ever-deeper red
And yellow and green, you pulled and
Stretched till the thin virgin cloth bled
Beneath the weight of so many
Clashing colours.

The white now bright and multicoloured
Quivers between two sets of poised
Hands and shivers as you twist and
Shape, gather into a knotted
Coil the colour-drenched, evanescent,
Sun-dried *dupattas*.

Stretch tightly and pull the taut threads.

Those were the early days when such
Jewelled, half-transparent veils
Shielded your eyes and your being
From the glaring daylight hours.
A shimmering self-enclosed world
Of trinkets and of secrets told
Only to girls not overbold
Beneath marriage-veils.

And as for you, too old a child,
Yet too young a woman, still new
To everything beyond the hearth,
You nightly dreamt that jasmine scents
Tempt fairies to whisk credulous

Young girls to distant magic lands.
Your prayers, they said, held promises
That all married women gain said.
You had the powers of an untouched
Fate and you were pure.

Your old bent head, now grey, presides
Over the kitchen, the family
News, the servants' chatter, plates of
Richly-spiced, long-stirred, vanishing
Food presented punctually at
Five. Dyeing *dupattas* and magic
Lands are now, years after, misty
Dreams firmly clasped, with iron bars,
To distant youth.

Stretch tightly and tear the taut threads.

But I, watching across the years
With newborn burning desire,
How can I, with body new,
Forbear to explore the world
Of brave endeavour, forbear to
Join the high green wave crashing
Resoundingly against the rocks
Of manly fortitude? I won't
Stand by, watching all men plunder
The wishes of my early youth.

Even now, decades later, I am
Not sure you understand that I,
Woman though I am, cannot be
Held back by that umbilical cord—
That lovely colour-splattered veil
Of yours that tugs to restrain me,
That pulls to hold me back from that
Compelling, violent urge within—
To break the taut threads, to shatter
The web of colour, to tear the
Nets of confusing cloth stretched tightly
About me.

AN ODE TO DEAD FLOWERS

*I*n the garish glare of shops reflecting
Undiluted sunshine, stare two pairs of
Eyes, hidden under fallen hair, two girls
About the size of half a lamp-pole. The
Garbage of yesterday's carousing lies
Scattered across their lives of cement
And begging bowls—crushed paper
Bags, lifeless, unnurturing scraps of
Buns half-eaten, mouldy popcorn
Kernels and empty ice cream cones.
Looming passersby with high heads
Against the sky look in front, not below
To two pairs of outstretched hands
And two pairs of wide eyes.

Their morning is spent amidst a scented
Garden, picking flowers. Warm earth-smells are
Gorgeously enhanced by the trailing
Strands of dead, pale, wrinkled roses, and the
White, petrified remains of huge and bloated
Narcissuses. The shop across the way,
Housing 'Floral Delights—All Kinds', has none
That can match theirs. Their paradise consists
Of yesterday's worn-out glory: their flowers,
Picked twice, are a second time immortal,
Resurrected from others' garbage heaps.

Dead flowers have the power to please
As any flushing, budding, growing weed
That unfurls its splendour-streaked petals
In lewd invitation. Amongst the refuse
Of the streets, lying helpless, is the purer

Seed of parents too poor to provide shelter.
Even nature's unwanted, cast-off leaves
Feed a better generation than fields
Of lusty, self-assertive greens.

A bouquet of roses that your lover keeps
For special days will waste away before
These drained remnants of nature's cycle.
Picked from society's begrudging streets
By children lovingly, you cannot say no.
Mischief-eyed, they peer into your garden of
Full-blown roses, and offer these: can you
Refuse as they extend their hands,
And beg you to buy so that they can eat?

THE RESURRECTION

*T*he restless cycle of birds
Tumbling endlessly from smoky treetops
Like fallen leaves in some absurd desert-autumn,
Echo and re-echo to the eye.
Swarming across cemented pavements,
Sweeping crumbs with frenzied wings until the next
Green light releases
Traffic from trance, noise from engines—
Together they move:
The passive leaves rise as resurrected,
Grow, expand with outstretched wings,
And in a breath, a moment's glance,
Compelled upwards,
Wearily climb towards their dusty heaven,
Wings folded, to pray and await
A carless, smokeless paradise.

AMIDST THE TRAFFIC

*P*eering through windows,
Each scene an artist's plate —
A social canvas in some dusty book,
The hidden secrets of a nation in pain.

We are driving through the streets of
Karachi.

*

At the traffic lights,
A young girl with a dark, charming face,
Head covered by a loosely draped, dirty *dupatta*
Looks at me with black eyes,
Thrusts towels against my window
And begs me to buy.
Refused,
She turns away, disappearing with faceless others,
Road-side gypsies
Ravenously consumed by the tangled throng.
The lights, like shifty chameleons, change colour
And we all move on.
I long to catch and question, embrace
This little girl selling towels, crowned with yellowed lace—
But she is left behind, counting, always counting,
Cheap towels by the roadside.

*

At a fruit stand, we pause.
Mangoes, melons, plums, apricots,
Heap after heap with dancing bananas in the sky.

85

The shopkeeper leaps, grabs cherries, weighs
And gives them to the lady in gray.
A truck pulls up with tumbling boys.
Wide mouths and elastic grins,
They jump out, stretching to catch
Oranges flung in their direction.
They hop about in dirt puddles, barefoot,
Tugging, pushing one another.
Sharp, pointed faces, dark bodies clothed in dark cloth.
A leap into their trucks and they are gone.
Orange peels lie on the road.

*

Old woman crossing the street—
Belly sagging, lined face and rotting teeth
Dark with stains of betel leaf.
Cars flash without cease—
No relief.
She waits, chewing, mulling over *paan*.
A bus blares, she retreats,
Alone by the side of the street, all alone.
Tall, lanky men like fresh blades
Of newly sprung grass,
While she, a weed awaiting the swing
Of a smart and shiny axe—
They zigzag and dash amidst ferocious,
Jungle-shaking, earth-quaking truck horns.
They cross, but she stands alone, chewing,
Waiting, waiting, anticipating…

*

Trucks full of heads with no before or after,
Steaming snouts still warm from
Inhaling, exhaling—breathing—now are shorn.
Passive, huge, hideous with flapping ears and
Eyes raised to heaven—How absurd, this herd of
Cruising, dead buffalo heads.

*

Paint a picture in the rain,
So colours run and blend,
Canvas and streets awash with muddy water.
Drops pure and clear, like messages from heaven—
Confused only as they hit the earth.
Small blue truck, half-beaten, old with frame behind,
No cover, naked beams of metal,
Cluttered, entwined
With men, suspended monkeys of the jungle,
Exuberantly yelling. Can you hear
The twice-removed bellowing of
Those men playing in the rain?

*

I long to capture these scenes and hang
Them up in a picture gallery with captions:
'A Girl in the Street,' 'The Beggar Man',
'I am Still Amidst the Movement and the Heat'—
Take living scenes and transpose them on moving film,
With the sounds, smells, the beat and emotions of
The people of the streets.
Don't fly away—
There is a certain peace in all your agitation.

BUY MY FLAG

*F*ourteenth of August.
A tribute to the boy who
Still sees the glamour of the flag
Through hard metal and
Eternally turning wheels,
Through dust and gas and grime,
Through choking fumes,
Exhausted.

Green and white, star-studded
Flags of independence
Fluttering like bunches of
Meaningless market wares.

Green and white, the colour of
Summer grass and jasmine,
Trees and icy river-foam,
Purity and peace
Contorted into someone else's
Dream of grasping a ten rupee note.

Buy my flag! Buy my flag
So that I can pull myself out of
Searing flames of engine heat
And hellish, gnawing need,
So I can cool my face,
Hide from the heavy weight
Of the immovable sun,
Retreat into some silent,
Full-stomached sleep
In a country of my own.

THE SUPPLICATION OF THE UNEMPLOYED CARPENTER

*C*rouched. Hands against head,
In supplication I sit before
The mosque, gazing dazedly at
Passing cars, shreds of coloured
Lightning. Coloured glass of
Broken bottles strewn
Dispassionately, listlessly by fate
Lie at my feet and near the gate
Of the eggshell-blue mosque.
O road of meandering ways,
How many days have I spent
Scouring your rough and stony
Face for sympathy? Graceless, you
Tear my limbs as I, barefoot,
Avoid the shattered rocks,
The sharp-toothedness of your
Shameless grin.

Crouched. Hands against heart,
In supplication I sit before the
Palely gleaming mosque of early
Morning mist. My dusty box of
Implements, desiring the heady
Sensuousness of touch, lies
Passive, frustrated of purpose.
O marketplace of shoddy wares,
How many days have I caressed your
Thorny thighs, expectant of
Fruitful recompense? Here am I,
Gazing dazedly at passing cars,
Waiting for a thousand doors
To open radiantly onto

A paradisal landscape:
Crippled chairs, collapsing
Tables longing for healthy limbs.

Wayfarer, solitary pilgrim praying
With hands against head,
Before the mosque, I wait,
Day by day. Dawn and dusk, the
Hours in between of aimless staring.
My path waylaid by the spectre of
Self-absorbed, uncaring,
Languishly satiated humanity.
Dawn and dusk, mosque, road, cars,
And horns blaring for easy passage
Through the softly rising dust.

I hold my head and wait.

THEOLOGICAL TOYS

Several whiplashes ago
i trembled with concern
at the rakishness of belief
i heard the call
but wondered who was calling

with each scar
sketched nicely across the body
i summoned wayward parts
of the soul to bear
evidence of my disbelief

i'm wiser now
and have learnt to live
neatly between the strokes
that fall with picket precision
on the wounded back of faith

in times to come
i'll watch the young ones play
with theological toys
burning their cute little palms
learning to make deals with God

NEUTER NIGHTS

The great sceptre hangs rigid
from the domes of pleasure
like an electric aqua-line chandelier

inside
all is still
a stillness
that death would envy

stewards of desire
come and go
like surfers on a sentient sea

inside
a silence so deep
that even widows would not weep

the obelisks of passion
stand tall beneath tremulous stars
while pigeon wings caress their tops

inside
a whisper that fails to form
an image that crumbles to the touch
a phantom that limps in the night
a thought that destroys all thought.

OVER THE EDGE BUT SANE

the earth was square
when mad men stood on edge
some slipped while others leapt
others still went around the bend
but i was yet a little sane

i would not really care
if the bleakish line were to stretch
from within to the deepest depth
as long as sailors could pretend
that they still weather sun and rain

one day i will have to dare
to cross the horizon to fetch
a few of the tears that were wept
by a young long lost friend
who suffered in silence her pain

NO MORE VOICES

i hear no more voices now
none that i would none
that talk to me none
that whisper proverbs
of tenderness none
that would carry
the old metaphysics of love

i hear no more voices now
neither from inside nor
from outside these realms
of conscience stark

voices that were
companions in the dark or
mates in daylight or
fellow travellers on the road
i hear them no more
in these caves of silence

voices that had gone
to husk words sundrenched
in hay no longer the touch
of shade nor the honeyed sun
neither tremor nor response
no waves that come and go
no shore upon which to lie

i hear no more voices now
only the beat of passing life

SIGNIFICANCE

Tomorrow spills over into yesterday when
the future reflects an unfathomable lie,
able to swallow one whole forever and
disrupt memories alive with pain—
causal surrender to cheap regrets.
Tears travel with perfect cohesion
into oblivion with complete awareness
shimmering halos adorned with dew,
cover timid hearts with shrouds of tenderness
drawn tight as if in mock embrace.
My listless eyes are prone to stare
at mysteries unveiling into nothingness,
a nothingness that grows miraculously
into a cloud that effortlessly drifts by.
Smiles become confused into sighs
and fields of clover lie breathless
with only the moon to eavesdrop
upon innocent thoughts from irrational minds.
There reality existed because it was denied,
and eventually succumbed to pestilence,
but for a while made all the difference.

SLIPPING AWAY

I feel you slip away,
fade into enveloping darkness
with the methodical passage
of each torturous second.
I reach out in desperation
stretch my arms to limit
but you merely pass through—
like a fistful of empty air
that one boasted tremendous potential
for a body grown cold.
Somewhere a muted heartbeat resounds
relentlessly performing its daily chores,
but no longer with uncorrupted passion.
A touch that once made me tingle
and twitch nervously like a child
now seems oppressive and heavy
leaving strains of deep regret wherever it touches.
I look into your distant eyes
and gasp upon seeing nothing
not even an ounce of casual reflection.
Visions of complacent indifference,
fresh fruit evolving into seeds
from the dampness of bitter tears.

MEDITATION

Funny the only
peace I get is in
hibernation
From the elements
of discord.
Curled up in a
ball of harnessed
agitation
Ready to unleash
another day on
the world.

TOTAL

Confidence in the
scope of the
enduring soul
is a weakness
in itself
Inspiring one to
take action
when it were
better to
watch and wait
and wander
in the endless
climes of the
burgeoning mind,
where many an idea
comes with the freshness of
a real discovery,
only to fade in the gentle afterglow
of a passive
acceptance of
non-change.

DILEMMA

Diamonds on my
fingers,
with a bankrupt
soul,
I collide with
reality,
in minute eruptions
of consciousness.

JUST BECAUSE

The truth itches,
Do you have to
scratch the
person beside you
After all,
plain speaking
is a
delicious liability
at the best of
times.

FORTUNA 501

$\mathcal{R}$ed tabbed, streamlined
you stroll down
the knee-jerked
highway
Hasn't anyone told you
that the owners of
Mercs are already
fortunate.

PARTICULARLY

empty is perhaps
a depth of non-feeling
An anaesthetized soul yearning
for freedom from pain
Missing the agony
as proof of feeling-
to- be.

SILENCE

Something within me calls out
and mingles into silence…
the answer emerges
but the quiet continues
like the sunrise
expanding without sound.
It overpowers the rest

and I become a part of that
silence.

POEM

The room is heavy with you again.
You scream out for me silently…
I will not come..

I know you
Your substance is ground into mine
I see you without sight
I hear you without sound.

You are always surprised—
This is the difference between us
You only know the beginning
I come from another life
I am pausing—only to pass on
I have been through everything
Before you.

SHIKARGAH[1]

I see your life
in a carpet
unrolled before me.
I see strange visions
in each colour
of this hunt

Your high climbs
and steep falls
each remoulding you
into the same creature
of circumstance

Your pride looming
dark and thick
murmuring
to the heights above

And some instinct
draws me to that web
around your person.
Your power over me
shall be my pillory.
It claws
like pain.
It sets a whirlpool going
in screams
sometimes loud
sometimes stifled.

---

1. Hunting scene woven into a carpet.

But you are lost
in time
your hold forsaken
along the voyage you undertook
which I have foreseen
in these colours
woven before me
now.

BLUR OF GLACIERS

A face buried in a bunch
of flowers;
a blur of glaciers
that break and fall;
an illness
that consumes, isolates
a worm that finds its path
till the insides are eaten.

A strange surprise
which is expectation
thought continuing
a landslide
rumbling down the mountains
that brings the traveller
to a stop.

But time is a mirror wiped clean;
and shells tossed on the beach
are gathered deep
amongst plants
thorny, purple and green

MOUNDS OF EARTH

Mounds of earth are thrown
spade by spade
on dust that will be
and with the seeping
of rain
green shoots sprout
and flowers
stare back

spirits hungering
for words
embossed
in each satiny petal
and graceful
bend of the neck

each dewdrop
echoing a story
piece by piece
in its meandering fall

statues speaking
of the power
of hands that shaped
countless times

of ideas ripened
in the smouldering furnace
of some mind

WANDERINGS

*T*he air of this dusty old city of mine
will change one day—
a tune that will escape
the strings of some harpsichord
playing in the woods in deep springtime.
A lingering essence of arrival murmuring
from each leaf trembling with soft raindrops
as if some shy creature for the wilderness
has traced its pattern of flight.

Silent, verdant trees
standing as gloomy ghosts—
Rhododendrons blossom in multitudes
of white, pink and purple—
an emotion that is the lightning
of mustangs at play.
Their long hair flowing in silver waves
into a valley of black mountains,
growing giants in the moonlight.

A man who will have wandered
through this world in search
of a face that bears a stamp
he can never forget;
which has become the flight
of a lone bird
along white peaks

WATERFALL ON BARE ROCKS

*H*e goes to the place he calls home
a solitary, bare room
with paint peeling off the walls
and clothes flying out of cupboards.
The mirror reflects a moustached face
staring back into eyes
strained with a madness.

He moves about
vaguely bruised
longing to crouch
in the damp shadows of some grove

The pleasure lies hidden
in that one powerful moment.
The rest flows out in a wild effusion—
the cool spray of a waterfall on bare rocks
flashing in the desert

But the windows are all shut.
The air is saturated
with him

CERTITUDE OF BEING

*D*o not try to understand me, all comprehension is
relative.
I am a page torn out of some ancient manuscript
streaked and yellowed with time.
It's flown wantonly
to fall and trace its path on the ground.
I have been set free
within oceans and seas.
I have lived amongst their strange creations
I have been part of their silent woes.

Come within my world.
Veil after veil will fall as you are led on
within intervals of serenity, rage and storm.
Each phase blurred by a vapour, a mist.

It may open a gateway for you, never fully shut
a streak of light always peers through.
Here there are no windows, not even prison bars
for a whiff to fresh air.
For the intruder there is no escape.
In these pathways there is no lightening
only scattered reflections of purple, blue and deep red.

And then one day, a fire will consume my physical state.
That will be the moment of your flight.
You will step upon my ashes and walk ahead
towards your light.

And I will simply drift
to merge into the infinity of time and space.
In this world of yours

one meets only to part at a destined moment.
But in this realm a union will occur
between the end and finished creations
of so many lives, so many centuries.

INDEX OF FIRST LINES

CONTRIBUTORS

Abbas Husain
Educated in Pakistan, he has a special calling for the cause of teacher training. A founder-member of SPELT (Society of Pakistan English Language Teachers) and a RSA-COTE tutor, he directs the Teachers' Development Centre in Karachi.

Athar Tahir
A Rhodes Scholar for Pakistan, 1974 at Oriel College where he read English Literature, he was also awarded the Hubert H. Humphrey Fellowship for study at the University of South Carolina. His critical reviews and translations from Urdu and Punjabi have been published widely. His work on a nineteenth century Punjabi poet, *Qadir Yar: A Critical Introduction*, won the Shah Abdul Latif Bhitai Award, 1990, and the National Book Council Prize, 1991. He is an elected Fellow of the Royal Asiatic Society of Great Britain.

Farida Faizullah
A graduate from the University of Karachi, she has taught at Abdullah Government College for Women. She has worked with SPELT and the British Council on various projects. She has translated poems from Urdu to English and her work is included in *Women's Writing—Pakistani Literature*, published by the Pakistan Academy of Letters.

Ghulam Fariduddin Riaz
He has attended the Fletcher School of Law and Diplomacy,Tufts University, Massachusetts. His first book, *Shade in Passing and Other Poems* was published by the Writers' Workshop, Calcutta in 1989. It was awarded the Patras Bokhari National Award for the Best Work in English, for the year 1992, by the Pakistan Academy of Letters. His other book, *Escaping Twenty Shadows*, was published in 1995.

Gulzar Bano
She has a Masters Degree in English Literature from the Punjab University. A member of the Pakistan Civil Service, she has trained in Holland, Canada and the US. Currently she is working for the uplift of communities at the grass roots level. Her poems have been privately published for circulation at the Beijing World Conference and NGO Forum for Women in 1995.

Mansoor Y. Sheikh
He has studied Pharmacy and Business Administration. During the 1970s and 1980s, he conducted various poetry readings and workshops. He was also the co-founder of *Mixed Voices*, a literary forum. His poetry has been published in anthologies in the UK (*Blue Wind: Poems in English from Pakistan*) and USA. His poem, *Intaglia* was awarded a Gold Medal in the All Nations Poetry Contest conducted by Triton College in Illinois.

Masood Amjad Ali
A Masters in English Literature from the University of Karachi, he was awarded a Postgraduate Diploma in English Studies from Leeds. He is professor and chairman of the Department of English Literature at the University of Karachi. He has read his poems at the Arts Council of Pakistan, and at literary gatherings at the University of Karachi and at Christ College, Cambridge.

Moeen Faruqi
A graduate from the California State University, he has also earned an M.Ed. Degree from the University of Wales, Cardiff. He is a journalist, school administrator, and an artist who has held several exhibitions all over Pakistan. His poems have been published both here and in the UK. His work has appeared in *Orbis*, *The Rialto* and *Iron*, England, *Verse*, Scotland, and *Cyphers*, Ireland.

Mona Hassan
She received both BA (Honours) and MA degrees from the University of Karachi. Currently a Lecturer at the Department of English, University of Karachi, she is also one of the founding members and the Secretary of The Shakespeare Association of Pakistan.

Nishat Wasim
An MA from the University of Karachi, she is a Lecturer in the Department, specializing in drama and poetry. Her poems have seen published in *Dawn, Women's Own, Pakistan Quarterly* and *Vision*. A founder member of The Shakespeare Association of Pakistan and an active member of SPELT, she writes poetry in English and Urdu.

Perveen Pasha
She has read English Literature and General History at the University of Karachi. Her poems have been published in several magazines and newspapers. Her first book, *Shades of Silence,* was published in early 1996.

Shahbano Bilgrami
She grew up in Montreal, Canada, where, three years in succession, she won both her school's annual Creative Writing Prize and first place in an annual provincial essay writing competition. She was also awarded the Founder's Prize by the Montreal Jewish Public Library for two short stories. She is currently working in Karachi and studying privately towards a BA degree in English from the London University.

Shahryar Rashed
He has studied at the UN International School in New York, the Drew University in Madison, the Punjab University, and briefly the Sorbonne in Paris. He has been published both at home and abroad, and is the author of a book of poems *Hybrid*, Almaab Printers, Lahore, 1991. He is also the author of a number of radio and stage plays performed by professional and amateur groups. He lectures on professional and literary subjects.

Sheryar Singha

Educated in Karachi and London, he now lives in Atlanta, USA, where he has also completed a degree in International Relations. Shehryar has recently started writing poetry.

Soofia Ishaque

She graduated Phi Beta Kappa in 1992 with a double major in English and Economics from Bowdoin College, Brunswick. She is working in an advertising agency, and is also a freelance journalist.

Zeba Hasan Hafeez

She is a dermatologist by profession. Her poetry has been included in the anthologies *The Glow Within*, *Portraits of Life* and *Firefly*, USA. She has also been published in several magazines in Pakistan, India and the USA. Recently nominated Poet of the Year for 1997 by the International Society of Poets, USA, she has been invited to attend their annual conference in Washington DC.